Barcode in back of Book

E
184
.J3
L4

Leathers, Noel L.

The Japanese in
America

THE JAPANESE IN AMERICA

The IN AMERICA *Series*

THE JAPANESE IN AMERICA

NOEL L. LEATHERS, Ph.D.

Published by

Lerner Publications Company

Minneapolis, Minnesota

1974 Revised Edition

Copyright © 1967 by Lerner Publications Company
International Copyright Secured. Printed in U.S.A.

International Standard Book Number: 0-8225-0211-9
Library of Congress Catalog Card Number: 67-15684

Second Printing 1968
Third Printing 1969
Fourth Printing 1971
Fifth Printing 1974

. . . CONTENTS . . .

Commodore Matthew C. Perry, as seen by a Japanese artist. Perry sailed into Tokyo Bay in 1853 and in the following year arranged a treaty with the Japanese which was the first to grant trading privileges to a Western nation.

PART I

The Background of Japanese Immigrants

1. *The Westernization of Japan*

The mention of Japan reminds most of us of Pearl Harbor, Hiroshima, Mount Fuji, judo, karate, and Tokyo. In fact, few of us probably know much more than this about the Japanese people and their country. We may know even less about the reasons that sent Japanese emigrants to America and the contributions they have made to our country.

The United States has played a unique role in the history of Japan and its people. It was an American naval officer, Commodore Matthew C. Perry, who introduced the Japanese to the Western World just a little over a century ago. Until that time, Japan had been isolated from the rest of the world for hundreds of years. For a long period of time, visitors were not allowed in the country, nor were the Japanese people allowed to leave their homeland.

In 1869, shortly after Commodore Perry convinced the Japanese to open their ports to American traders, Emperor Meiji became the absolute sovereign of Japan. Almost at once he began to modernize his nation by sending Japan's most intelligent young men throughout the world to learn the ways of the West. They went to nearly every modern nation on the globe, including the United States, Great Britain, Germany, France, and Russia. From each of these nations the Japanese borrowed those things which they thought would be most useful to them. The sewage and sanitation system of the city of Philadelphia was adopted for Japanese urban centers; the constitution of Japan was borrowed in general from that of Prussia. In a few years, the Japanese transformed their nation from a backward medieval country into a thriving modern industrial state.

Although modernization brought many advances to Japan, it also brought problems. The country of Japan consists of four main islands: Hokkaido, Honshu, Kyushu, and Shikoku. The amount of land in Japan suitable for farming is only 14 percent of the total land area. This is because there are many mountain ranges and stretches along the coasts which are unfit for farming. Once Japan began to modernize, the population of the nation increased rapidly and the problem of finding enough food became more severe than ever before. Therefore, many Japanese began to look overseas for a place to live.

The modernization of Japan meant that many factories were built. These industrial plants needed large supplies of raw materials for manufacturing. They also required fuel to operate their machinery. As a result, the natural resources of the homeland were severely taxed and it was found that Japanese iron and oil reserves were very limited. It became necessary for the Japanese Government to purchase or acquire land where these important materials were easily available. These efforts led to a series of wars and skirmishes with China and Russia around the 1900's. The victories won by Japan in these struggles served to strengthen the power and prestige of the military leaders who were gaining more and more influence in making government policy.

2. *The Reasons for Emigration*

Many Japanese objected to the modernization of Japan. Some were opposed to building big factories. Some disliked the monotony of working in dreary establishments as slaves to machinery. Others did not want to take part in wars or to serve in the army or navy. Still others were deeply concerned over the rise of military leaders and the glorification of ideas of force and might. For these and other reasons, many Japanese people decided that they should leave their homeland.

Other Japanese decided to emigrate for economic reasons. The growing population meant that land was becoming more and more scarce. It was increasingly difficult to produce enough food to meet their needs. Many Japanese families made their living by farming a plot of ground no larger than 30 feet wide and 100 feet long. Those that came and settled in America considered their small farms of 10 and 20 acres "ranches" compared to their old landholdings in Japan.

American troops in the temple grounds at Simoda, Japan, June 8, 1854. Perry impressed the Emperor's commissioners with his dignified behavior and his elaborate displays of troops.

Low wages also encouraged many Japanese to emigrate. Japanese workers had not learned the art of organizing unions and other groups to improve their working conditions, hours, and pay. The expansion of trade had given Japanese trade delegations and representatives opportunities to travel abroad. Japanese businessmen, officials, and seamen thus became aware of the opportunities in foreign lands. They saw the better economic conditions that existed outside Japan and so became interested in emigrating.

3. *The Japanese People*

The Japanese people who came to America had many different customs and beliefs compared to people of other immigrant groups. Few Americans understood the Japanese way of life. Thus, the Japanese immigrants met with much prejudice and distrust in America.

The Japanese believe that their country is truly the land of the rising sun. In Japanese folklore, the great sun-goddess, O-me-kame-Ameterasu, descended from the heavens in ancient times and created the Japanese homeland. The Japanese believe that their emperors are direct descendants of this sun-goddess and thus, are divine.

In addition to worshipping their emperor as divinity, the Japanese, like many other Oriental peoples, have a great respect for the elder members of their families. The Shinto religion strengthens this practice by encouraging the construction of public and private shrines and altars to the dead. This great respect for the wisdom of the older generation is a trait which is deeply ingrained into most Asiatic societies. Although the customs of the Japanese people have changed considerably since World War II, many of the earlier ways were brought to America by the Japanese who came before the war.

Shinto shrine at Ise. The Shinto religion, which originated with the worship of nature gods, also teaches honor and respect of one's elders, living or dead.

Business center of the Japanese section, Los Angeles, 1907.

PART II

Japanese Immigration to America

The first Japanese to come to the United States were accidental visitors who were the victims of shipwrecks on the high seas. There were several incidents of this kind in the 1850's, which was about the same time that Commodore Perry was gaining privileges for shipwrecked American sailors in Japan. The number of Japanese immigrants, however, grew very slowly. By 1880 there were not more than 150 in the United States. Only in 1885 did the Japanese Government pass laws permitting its people to emigrate. From that time on, the number of Japanese in America increased very rapidly. During the decade of the 1890's, the annual average was slightly more than 1,000. In 1900, more than 12,000 Japanese immigrants entered the United States.

1. *Reasons for Increased Immigration*

There were two major reasons for the sudden increase in Japanese immigration. The Chinese Exclusion Act of 1882 stopped the immigration from China to America. This was passed because of the concern over Chinese labor flooding the market and leaving no jobs for Americans. The result of the act, however, was a labor shortage in the western part of our country. This was particularly true in California, and many California farmers were eager to bring in foreign laborers to work in their fields. Thus, there was a demand for Japanese immigrants who were good farm laborers and who would work for low wages.

Another factor which helped stimulate Japanese immigration was a law passed by the Japanese Government in 1896. This Emigrants Protection Law required that each departing worker have someone responsible for his financial support so that if he became ill or unable to work, he would not suffer. Through this law, the Japanese Government intended to make sure that any of its people who emigrated would be well taken care of regardless of where they traveled. The restrictions and financial requirements of this law were so strict that most Japanese families could not afford to support an emigrant to the United States. As a result, a number of emigration companies sprang up in Japan in cooperation with labor contractors in the United States. These emigration companies furnished the Japanese emigrant with the necessary financial assistance and guaranteed him a job when he reached the United States.

The emigration companies were a huge success. Between 1899 and 1904, nearly 60,000 Japanese came to America, excited by the stories of wealth and higher wages made in the United States. Special notices were displayed in Japanese villages describing the great advantages of California and encouraging young Japanese men to sign up for a job there. From 1900 to 1905, nearly 20,000 Japanese were attracted to California. These companies were also at work in Hawaii.

Officials of the first Japanese Embassy to the United States, 1860. In this drawing, Ambassador Shimmi is seated at the left.

2. *The Life of Japanese Immigrants in America*

Unfortunately, many found that the stories of the great wealth and the wonderful life in the United States were greatly exaggerated. New immigrants who came under the authority of an emigration company were lined up as soon as they stepped off their ship and marched off in military fashion to the company's barracks. From there they were assigned to California farmers as laborers. Others who came to the west coast on their own found it necessary to seek the company of earlier immigrants in order to learn the ways of their new nation.

In most instances, unskilled workers became agricultural laborers. They worked for lower wages than native Americans who were

Farm near Shizuoka, Japan. Scarcity of land to raise crops for a growing population was one reason for emigration.

Fishing boats, Los Angeles Harbor. Japanese fishermen settled on Terminal Island in 1901, established canneries, and eventually had a thriving industry.

performing the same kind of work. Skilled craftsmen went to live in the cities. Soon sections known as "Little Tokyos" sprang up in most of the west coast towns. Since the new immigrants had little money, it was necessary for them to find inexpensive housing. They were usually forced to rent in areas which were not very desirable. Their living quarters were often crowded, dark, and had insufficient sanitary facilities.

The types of work which the Japanese found varied greatly. Farming, merchandising, domestic service, railways, factory work, canneries, dairying, plant nurseries, fisheries, and clerical tasks claimed most of the new immigrants. By 1920, however, there were also more than 350 Japanese-Americans gainfully employed as professionals—doctors, lawyers, dentists, and professors.

Most Japanese immigrants were young men between the ages of 20 and 40. Until the end of World War I, young Japanese men outnumbered young Japanese women among the immigrants three to one. Because of this, many a Japanese young man decided to marry a girl from Japan and bring her to his new home in the United States.

15

Since a young Japanese immigrant in America did not have the money to travel to Japan and then return with a new bride, a practice developed which became known as a "picture bride" marriage. The young immigrant would write a letter back home to his parents telling them that he would like to marry a suitable young Japanese girl. Many times he would ask his parents to make the proposal to a girl in his hometown whom he had known before coming to the United States. His parents took this responsibility very seriously. They made extensive inquiries into the family, training, manners, and general character of the girl of their son's desires. The bride's parents were equally concerned about their future son-in-law and they, too, would make numerous checks upon his family. If everything turned out to be satisfactory, the marriage ceremony would be performed in Japan with the bride dressed in her finest and the groom's family representing the young immigrant in America.

Once the marriage was officially performed in Japan, the Japanese Government would permit the new bride to leave her homeland to join her new husband in the United States. Many times the young immigrant would meet his bride at the dock and then go through another marriage ceremony in accordance with the custom of his new homeland. Since the marriage negotiations often involved an exchange of pictures between the two families, many Americans dubbed these ceremonies "picture bride" marriages. This marriage custom, which seemed strange to many Americans, helped build prejudice against Japanese immigrants. In 1920 the Japanese Government announced that it would discontinue issuing passports to so-called "picture brides" because of the bitterness of American citizens who were anti-Japanese.

The Japanese immigrants that came to America often referred to themselves as *issei* or *nisei*. Issei (pronounced *ee-sayee*) means that the person was born in Japan and therefore is a first generation immigrant to this country. Nisei (pronounced *nee-sayee*) means that the person is an immigrant's son or daughter who was born in the United States. Thus, a nisei is a native-born American. Since further immigration from Japan was prohibited under the Immigration Act of 1924, there are very few issei still living today. Most Americans

Immigration station of the Department of Labor, Honolulu, 1918. Japanese immigrants await examination.

of Japanese ancestry whom you meet are therefore nisei, or the children of nisei.

3. *Agriculture and the Japanese Immigrant*

Nearly 50 percent of the new Japanese immigrants became farm workers. Most of the immigrants had come from small villages and rural areas in Japan where farming was the chief way of earning a living. In addition, Japan had been a predominantly agricultural nation throughout most of its long history. In some areas of the United States there was a severe shortage of farm laborers. New immigrants were welcomed by the farm contractors who were quick to see that the Japanese were excellent workers and excelled at many tasks concerned with the planting and harvesting of crops. In other areas, many white farmers objected to the new immigrants, arguing that since the Japanese worked for lower wages, they could not compete with them in selling their produce.

Harvesting strawberries in Gardena, California, 1911. Entire families worked in the fields.

The Japanese soon made up a significant portion of the farm labor supply on the west coast. More than half of the citrus and deciduous fruits were produced by Japanese labor and more than 90 percent of the vegetables, berries, and grapes were under the control of Japanese contractors and farm workers. The Japanese were able to compete successfully with white American contractors because in most instances, every member of the immigrant's family worked in the fields along with the men. Although their homes were often little more than shacks, the patient backbreaking toil in the fields seven days each week made it possible for these families to improve their standards of living within a remarkably short period of time.

Many Japanese immigrants who landed almost penniless at San Francisco were able to become landholders within a very few years. By 1920, the new immigrants owned nearly 75,000 acres and leased more than 383,000 acres. It is interesting to note that the average immigrant farm consisted of only 56 acres as compared to 320 acres of the average west coast farm. In spite of smaller farms, Japanese immigrants contributed 13 percent of the total agricultural produce of California. The majority of these products came from the Sacramento Valley where many immigrants had settled. The 1920 census figures showed that the Japanese population of California was slightly less than 110,000, or about 3 percent of the total population of the state.

The process of becoming a landowner was a difficult one for the

Japanese. The California legislature had passed a land law which was intended to prevent foreigners who were ineligible for citizenship from buying and holding titles to land. The citizenship laws of the United States at that time stated that only "white men and Africans" were eligible for citizenship. Thus, the Japanese were excluded from citizenship and landownership. In order to get around the provisions of the California land law, many immigrants purchased farmland in the name of their children, who were citizens of the United States because they had been born in this country.

Not only did the new immigrants seek to become substantial landholders and farmers in their own right by leasing farmlands, but they also formed organizations to promote their interests in their new country. More than 50 local associations sprang up in California alone. These soon formed the Japanese Agricultural Association of Southern California and the California Farmers Cooperative. These groups in turn became associated with the Japanese Association of America which had its headquarters in San Francisco. The Japanese Association of America was organized to promote the welfare of Japanese-Americans and to protect their rights and privileges. It also performed important work in bringing about closer friendship between the people of Japan and the United States.

The issei and nisei worked very hard at making a success of their lives in the New World. Stories of their industrious nature and successful struggles to overcome severe handicaps were widespread. Many considered the Japanese-Americans to be the best farmers in the entire nation. The story of Vacaville, California is one of many success stories.

Farm workers and their homes, 1911.

Vacaville had originally been settled by immigrants from one of the Scandinavian countries, but because of the adverse climate and soil conditions it had nearly become a ghost town. Several Japanese farm families decided to move to Vacaville because they could not buy or lease land where the climate was satisfactory and the soil fertile. Undoubtedly, many white Americans and even other Japanese immigrants laughed at them. Vacaville has an extremely hot climate. It was almost like a desert, with blowing sand and few plants hardy enough to survive such rigors.

The Japanese families that settled in the Vacaville area were determined to make something out of this barren wasteland. They brought in fertilizer and used it several times each year. They planted fruit trees and sprayed them over and over again instead of the usual once per season. They developed irrigation channels and supplied this farmland with four or five times more water than it had ever had before. With patient toil and backbreaking care, every member of these families worked at improving the soil and bringing in good crops. It was almost a miracle to outsiders who came to Vacaville. Within five years the barren wasteland had been transformed into one of the most profitable farming regions in the entire state of California. Similar stories could be told about the Imperial Valley and the areas in central California.

4. *The Fishing Industry*

While many Japanese were establishing their reputations as excellent farmers, other Japanese immigrants were using their skills in the fishing industry. One of the fishing centers was Terminal Island in Los Angeles Harbor. In 1901 a dozen Japanese abalone fishermen came to Terminal Island. They built their homes on stilts driven into the water along the shore. Their business grew so rapidly that by 1910 there were 3 fish canneries operating on the island and the population had reached 3,000. While the men went out in the fleets to fish, the women, children, and older men worked in the canneries cleaning and packing fish.

Most of the men fished for tuna and sardines. Sardine fishing was done at night when the fish were spotted by their reflection at the water's surface. At the first break of dawn the fishing fleet would race back to the harbor to unload at the cannery. The sardine fleets were ordinarily gone only overnight. The tuna fishing fleet, on the other hand, was usually gone for a period of a few days to two weeks. It covered extensive areas of the Pacific Ocean from Central America to Hawaii. By the beginning of World War II, 60 percent of the population of Terminal Island was of Japanese ancestry and was furnishing the supplies of seafood needed by the large metropolitan area of Los Angeles.

5. *Marketing*

Marketing, too, became a major occupation for the Japanese-Americans. They often concentrated their efforts in the wholesale produce industry. By 1940, Japanese-Americans accounted for roughly half of the total produce business of the major cities on the west coast. Some Japanese-Americans went into the wholesale business in order to furnish an outlet for the farm produce of their fellow farmers who sometimes were affected by boycotts. In this way, the Japanese-Americans gradually came to control certain crops (celery, peas, lettuce, and other vegetables) from the time they were planted until they were sold to the retailer or consumer. Many of the business transactions between Japanese-Americans were handled by word of mouth rather than by written contracts. It was understood that if one made a promise he would live up to his word.

Hawaiian tuna fishermen at lunch. Their boat is a power-driven sampan.

6. *The Shift in Population*

The diligence of the immigrants during the 1920's and 1930's helped to relieve much of the racial tension that resulted in the 1924 Immigration Act. The overwhelming majority of the Japanese continued to live on the west coast. During the 1930's, there was a gradual shift from rural to urban centers. Since World War II there has been a steady increase in the number of Japanese-Americans moving to other parts of the United States.

The motives pulling many nisei from the west coast to other parts of the United States are similar to those which attracted their parents from Japan earlier in the century. Greater economic gain plus a greater variety of opportunities are major factors in inducing many Japanese to seek new homes in the north central and northeastern sections of the nation. The median of education attained by those in the East is generally greater than on the west coast. The median in New York, for example, is 15 years and 3 months; but the same figure in California is 12 years 8 months. This reflects the presence of many professional people in the north central and northeastern parts of the country. It is not surprising, therefore, to discover that the average income of Japanese-Americans in the East is $500 per year higher than on the west coast.

Similarly, just as the early immigrants from Japan were usually young people, this is true of the movement across state lines within the United States. Half of those living east of the Rocky Mountains are under 35 years of age, and three-fourths are under 44 years. On the other hand, 78 percent of those over 70 years of age live in the western states.

Since World War II Japanese-Americans have concentrated in the major cities. Only seven percent in California now reside and work in agricultural areas. Oregon has nearly one-fourth of its Japanese-Americans living in rural areas, which is the highest proportion of any state in the nation. In the coastal states many continue to work in the fishing industry although they have moved to the urban centers. The majority of urbanites are engaged in jobs typical of most Americans. Among them are clerks, salesmen, foremen in factories, service workers, and craftsmen. Others are involved in manufacturing and professional and managerial positions. The percentage of Japanese-Americans involved in government work is low compared to other national groups.

7. *Contributions of Japanese-Americans*

Since World War II, the Japanese-Americans have achieved national recognition. One can hardly travel through the country today without seeing the work or influence of the distinguished Japanese-American architect, Minoru Yamasaki. Yamasaki was born in Seattle in 1912. He graduated from the University of Washington in 1934 and continued his studies at New York University. He has been

Temple of the North Shore Congregation Israel in Glencoe, Illinois. Designed by Japanese-American architect Minoru Yamasaki.

awarded numerous plaques and distinguished honors for his outstanding architectural designs. Among his many works are the Reynolds Metals Company Building in Detroit, the Public Housing Development in St. Louis, and the Oberlin College Music Conservatory Structure. He is probably best known for his work at the World's Fair held in Seattle in 1962. In 1956 he received the first honor award from the American Institute of Architects for his work and designs at the St. Louis Airport. In 1964 he was designated as the architect for a special project to be constructed near Disneyland, south of Los Angeles, California. This is to be a 170-acre, $100,000,000 realty development called "The City." Yamasaki has also designed the Woodrow Wilson School of Public and International Affairs for Princeton University and the noted Northwestern National Life Insurance Company building in Minneapolis. His buildings combine what may be described as the classical style of Greece merged with modern functional design and the influence of the Orient. Most of his structures are white and are built with quartz or marble. Mr. Yamasaki now makes his home in Birmingham, Michigan.

The Northwestern National Life Insurance Company. Built in 1963-64, this graceful building dominates a redeveloped area in downtown Minneapolis, Minnesota.

Minoru Yamasaki in front of the Northwestern National Life Insurance Company.

One of the most promising young conductors in the world of music is Seiji Ozawa. He was born in Japan in 1935, but he left for Europe in 1959 to study conducting. There he was seen by Leonard Bernstein of the New York Philharmonic Orchestra; Bernstein named Ozawa his assistant conductor for the 1961-62 season. From 1965 to 1969, Ozawa was the conductor of the Toronto Symphony, and in 1968, he was named conductor and musical director of the San Francisco Symphony Orchestra. Frequently, Seiji Ozawa is guest-conductor of the major symphony orchestras in the United States and Europe.

Isamu Noguchi is a world famous sculptor. He was born in Los Angeles, attended Columbia University, and studied in various parts of the world including Paris and China. He has worked in England, Mexico, and in other nations. One of his best known works in the United States is the relief sculpture for the Associated Press Building in Rockefeller Center. He also designed works for the New York World's Fair in 1939 and had one-man shows in nearly every major art gallery in the United States. His works today are scattered from New York, to Hawaii, to the Far East. In 1964 Mr. Noguchi was called in as a consultant for the design of the tomb in Arlington National Cemetery for the late John F. Kennedy.

Relief sculpture by Isamu Noguchi. Associated Press Building, Rockefeller Center, New York.

Noguchi receives the Fine Arts Medal from President Henry L. Wright of the American Institute of Architects, 1963.

Makoto Sakamoto, Olympic gymnast, and **Tommy Kono,** Olympic weight-lifter.

In the field of athletics, the Japanese-Americans have made their mark as well. Makoto Sakamoto, then a high school student, led the United States Men's Olympic Gymnastic Squad in the Tokyo Olympics in 1964. Tommy Kono, a health food salesman from Hawaii, competed in various weight lifting contests for over 15 years. He broke no less than 26 world records and won 8 world and 8 national titles. He won Olympic weight lifting titles for the United States in 1952 and 1956.

One of the best known Japanese-Americans in the academic world is Professor Henry Tatsumi. Professor Tatsumi is a specialist in the field of the Japanese language. During World War II, he contributed greatly to the war effort by instructing officers of the United States Navy at the Japanese language school located in Boulder, Colorado.

Another scholar of outstanding note is Professor John Maki. Professor Maki received his doctoral degree from Harvard University in 1948. He is an expert on government and politics of the Japanese nation.

As Japanese-Americans make their marks in other fields, it is natural that they should achieve recognition in the field of politics as well. In 1971, Norman Y. Mineta was elected mayor of San Jose, California, a city of over 450,000. Mr. Mineta is the first Japanese-American elected to an office of this rank in the state of California.

Professor Henry S. Tatsumi and **Professor John Maki.** Tatsumi teaches Japanese, and Maki is an expert on Japanese government and politics.

The achievement of these outstanding individuals and countless others, too numerous to mention, demonstrates the acceptance of Japanese-Americans in our society. However, the way to acceptance has not been easy, as we shall see in Part III.

Dr. Samuel Ichyle Hayakawa, president of San Francisco State College. Dr. Hayakawa assumed the presidency after severe student disorders forced the resignation of Robert R. Smith in November, 1968. An expert in languages, Dr. Hayakawa has written two books on the subject and formerly served as an English professor at the College.
(Courtesy San Francisco State College)

Mayor Eugene Schmitz of San Francisco and **Abraham Ruef,** his political boss. They used the strife between native Americans and Japanese immigrants to cover up their own corruption.

PART III

The Problem of Prejudice

The first instance of open hostility against the Japanese-Americans occurred in San Francisco shortly after the beginning of this century. At this time San Francisco was governed by Mayor Eugene E. Schmitz and his political boss, Abraham Ruef. The Schmitz-Ruef administration of San Francisco (1901-1906) was one of the most corrupt city governments in the history of the United States. When these men were finally placed under attack for corruption in office, they tried to use the Japanese-Americans as scapegoats to divert public attention from themselves.

Mayor Schmitz had been elected with the support of the Union Labor Party, which objected to competition from immigrant labor, particularly the Japanese-Americans. The Union Labor Party claimed that the new immigrants worked for lower wages and were driving native Americans out of their jobs. As a result of these complaints, the Japanese Government announced in 1900 that it would restrict the number of passports issued to persons wishing to come to the United States. Despite this action, many Japanese received passports, traveled to Hawaii, and came to the United States later. This meant that more and more immigrants were arriving at the very time hostility was developing in San Francisco.

Another factor which contributed to the anti-Japanese sentiment in the western states was the outbreak of the Russo-Japanese War in 1904. The rapid success of Japanese military forces in this conflict and the eventual seizure of Korea by Japan made many Americans fearful of the so-called "Yellow Peril," or the threat of Oriental people to the living standards and power of Western civilization. Fears were expressed that the west coast would be flooded with a wave of new Japanese immigrants at the end of the war with Russia. American laboring groups were worried that their jobs would be endangered. Finally, in 1905, there was a violent outbreak against the Japanese.

The Japanese-Americans were accused of forcing shoe repair men out of employment; of underbidding construction jobs by more than half; of controlling most of the manual laboring forces on the

President Theodore Roosevelt with envoys from Russia and Japan, August 5, 1905. Roosevelt brought them together at Portsmouth, New Hampshire to sign a treaty ending the Russo-Japanese War.

railroads in California. These charges were false, but there were many who believed them. *The San Francisco Chronicle,* the city's leading newspaper, ran front-page articles discussing the danger of additional immigration from Japan and Hawaii. The *Chronicle* charged the Japanese-Americans with maintaining loyalty to Emperor Meiji of Japan. It insisted that the immigrant children were crowding American children out of the classrooms in San Francisco school buildings.

With the urging of the *Chronicle,* the laboring groups in San Francisco began an all-out attack against the Japanese-Americans. A citywide boycott was started against Japanese merchants; mass meetings were held at which the immigrants were denounced as evil men who were undermining the United States. Some incidents of outright assault upon individual immigrants took place. The aroused native Americans were demanding that the national government adopt a policy of excluding the Japanese from the United States. Congressmen from California introduced an exclusion bill into Congress. President Theodore Roosevelt, however, was greatly opposed to this bill and said that he would veto any law excluding the Japanese, even if it passed Congress unanimously.

Roosevelt was strongly criticized in the west coast papers, but his strong statements killed the hope of the exclusionists for a time. Great events, however, were soon to revive the opposition.

At the height of this quarrel, San Francisco experienced its worst disaster in history, the great earthquake and fire of April 18, 1906. The Japanese-Americans contributed nearly $250,000 to the Red Cross for the relief of victims of the disaster. More than 10,000 Japanese-Americans had been affected by the fire and they were faced with the problem of finding new homes. They moved into districts which had previously been lived in only by white Americans. This added more fuel to the flames of racial prejudice. Following the earthquake and fire, San Francisco witnessed a major crime wave. The Japanese suffered robberies and violence along with other inhabitants of the bay area. Japanese stores were looted and leading Japanese figures were often victims of rock-throwing gangs.

1. *Discrimination and Education*

In 1906 the San Francisco school board directed all children of Japanese immigrants to attend a special school in Chinatown. The Japanese Association of America immediately protested this order. They pointed out that the Japanese children were not located in any one section of the city and that it would be impossible for them to attend the special school. The Japanese Government also protested against this form of discrimination. President Roosevelt described the board's action as a "wicked absurdity."

The facts of the situation show that there was no reason for the action of the school board. Out of a total enrollment of 25,000, there were only 93 Japanese students attending the San Francisco schools. A survey of the schools in San Francisco taken only a few months before had shown that there was no overcrowding. Another false claim widely publicized by the anti-Japanese was that many older Japanese were attending school with much younger white children. Actually, there were only two immigrants over 20 years of age attending schools, and they were there to learn the language of their new country.

Theodore Roosevelt opposed attempts to exclude the Japanese and to discriminate against them.

The San Francisco earthquake and fire, 1906, as seen by an artist for *Harper's Weekly*. Violence and disorder added to the difficulties already faced by Japanese-Americans at this time.

Many leading educators in California and other parts of the nation spoke out in opposition to the San Francisco school board. It was pointed out that not one single protest against the Japanese students had ever been filed with the school board by anyone. Early in 1907, President Roosevelt requested that board members come to Washington for discussions. Consequently, they reversed their decision and abolished the order. As part of the bargain, the President agreed to limit the immigration of Japanese from Hawaii into the United States. Agitation still continued, however, because the number of immigrants coming to the United States directly from Japan was increasing greatly.

2. *The Gentlemen's Agreement and Anti-Japanese Legislation*

In 1908, after an exchange of diplomatic notes with the United States, Japan agreed to voluntarily restrict further emigration. This was known as the Gentlemen's Agreement. Actually this agreement only prohibited the immigration of Japanese laborers into this country. The immigration of professional people from Japan was still permitted. As a result of this agreement, the flow of immigrants from Japan was cut to a minimum and the violent agitation on the west coast lessened for awhile. This was only a temporary letdown, however, and soon there were widespread demands voiced by agricultural groups to stop the Japanese from acquiring land.

In 1913 the legislature of California passed a law prohibiting Japanese from owning land. The vote in the state legislature was so overwhelmingly in favor of the law that the governor had no choice but to sign it. This Alien Land Act of 1913 also limited the length of land leases to three years. It was the intent of this law to discourage the number of immigrants coming into California. By 1920 the people of California voted to remove even the right of the Japanese to lease land.

It should be pointed out that the actions of the State of California were in direct opposition to the national government. President Wilson sent Secretary of State William Jennings Bryan to California in an effort to prevent passage of the law. However, the legislature, influenced by the agitation against the Japanese, ignored the pleas of the Washington officials.

The Japanese immigrants protested bitterly against these laws and charged that they were being denied equal protection of the law as guaranteed in the 14th Amendment to the Constitution of the United States. The various fruitgrower associations and the American Legion of California, however, insisted that Japanese-Americans represented a threat to the white race in America and that they should be prevented from owning land and bringing in more of their countrymen. These attacks upon the Japanese-American farmers were totally unjust, as some white Americans pointed out, but to no avail.

34

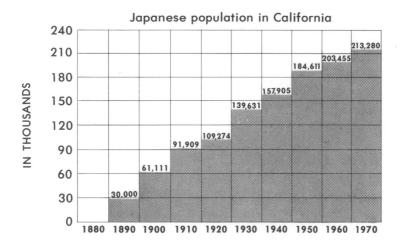

Japanese population in California

The final success of the anti-Japanese forces on the west coast came with the passage of the Immigration Act of 1924 by the Congress of the United States. Without mentioning the Japanese by name, this law provided for their total exclusion by refusing entry to aliens ineligible for United States citizenship. At that time, only people who were white or Negro were eligible for citizenship. This insult to the Japanese caused a great diplomatic furor and President Coolidge signed the bill with deep regret. He stated that if the measure had been only an anti-Japanese measure, he would have vetoed it. So great was the pressure of public opinion at the time,

President Calvin Coolidge reluctantly signed the bill which ended most Japanese immigration.

however, that he signed the bill. Japanese immigration then virtually stopped. There were still a few Japanese permitted to enter for family reasons or because of a special profession that they practiced.

The Immigration Act of 1924 brought to a head the anti-Japanese agitation which had begun in 1900. First, the Gentlemen's Agreement had been voluntarily practiced by the Government of Japan. Then, immigrants were prohibited from attending schools. Later, they were limited in their rights to purchase land or lease land for farming. These actions made the Japanese-Americans "second-class citizens."

Japanese food market, Los Angeles. Marketing is a major occupation of Japanese-Americans, a natural outgrowth of the farming and fishing industries.

Bombing of the *Panay*, a United States gunboat in the Yangtze River, China. This unprovoked raid by Japanese planes in 1937 intensified anti-Japanese feeling in America.

PART IV

Wartime Treatment

Had history not taken the course it did from 1931, Japanese-Americans may have been able to win complete acceptance in this country earlier. Events in the far Pacific, however, soon placed the entire position of the immigrants in danger, particularly on the west coast. In 1931 Japan invaded Manchuria and the United States Government reacted strongly to this action. In 1934 Japan withdrew from the League of Nations and scrapped an international treaty in which she had agreed to limit the size of her navy. By 1937 Japan had invaded China itself. American public opinion was inflamed against the aggressive intentions of the Empire of Japan. The destruction of the city of Nanking in December 1937, the sinking of an American gunboat, the *Panay*, and tales of atrocities committed by Japanese soldiers caused public feelings against Japan to mount rapidly in the United States. Soon the United States Government stopped oil shipments to Japan and relations between the two nations steadily worsened.

1. *Fear of Japanese Immigrants Mounts*

The Japanese-Americans living in this country became, of course, the target of many groups which were nursing old complaints and grievances against them. All of the old arguments about unfair competition, loyalties to the Japanese Emperor, and the supposedly evil influence that the "yellow race" was exerting upon white children were brought out and used again. Letters to the editors of west coast newspapers attacked the Japanese-Americans as being possible spies and saboteurs for the Empire of Japan. Poisonous statements began pouring forth from various organizations which aimed at destroying the Japanese settlements. As early as 1935, the following statement was issued by the Southern California Committee of One Thousand:

> Wherever the Japanese have settled, their nests pollute the communities like the running sores of leprosy. They exist like the yellowed, smoldering discarded butts in an over-full ashtray, villifying the air with their loathsome smells, filling all who have misfortune to look upon them with a wholesome disgust and a desire to wash.

Such statements are excellent examples of propaganda intended to excite public opinion without regard for the truth.

The flagship USS "Pennsylvania" and two destroyers. Pearl Harbor, Honolulu.

Explosion of the USS "Shaw," Pearl Harbor, December 7, 1941. Later that day Japan declared war against the United States and Great Britain.

The attack on Pearl Harbor on December 7, 1941, resulted in demands that all Japanese-Americans, whether citizens or not, be removed from the west coast because they represented a military danger to the United States. Some organizations declared that there were at least 25,000 Japanese civilians who were actually soldiers loyal to Japan. With the Japanese invasion of the west coast, these organizations declared, the Japanese-Americans would throw off their regular clothes and put on their hidden uniforms. Because of the Pearl Harbor attack and the steady gains won by the Japanese military forces in the Pacific during the first months of the war, many Americans were ready to believe almost any story about Japanese-Americans.

Many organizations were willing to go on record as favoring the complete removal of the Japanese from the west coast to concentration camps for the duration of the war. Other groups advised the government to ship all Japanese-Americans back to Japan after the war. These organizations included Chambers of Commerce from large cities, Farm Bureau groups, American Legion posts, the Native Sons and Daughters of the Golden West, and various businessmen's fraternal organizations. They all contributed to the pressure exerted on the national government.

Many of these groups encouraged their members to write letters to their Congressmen. Yet, the final count of letters received showed that there were fewer letters of protest against the Japanese than there had been against the Selective Service Act of 1940.

Nevertheless, the situation was tense. On January 31, 1942, California Governor Culbert Olson issued an order revoking the business licenses of 5,000 Japanese aliens. Earl Warren, who was then attorney general of California, stated that hundreds of Japanese organizations were to be wiped out and that all truck farmers who farmed on land within the vicinity of naval, army, and air force installations would be ousted. Mr. Warren went on to say that one could not tell the difference between a good Japanese-American and a bad one. Governor Arthur B. Langlie of Washington and Governor Charles A. Sprague of Oregon advised that they were keeping close watch on the situation in their states. Washington and Oregon combined, however, had fewer than 30,000 Japanese-Americans at this time, and the tension was considerably less than in California.

Recognizing the threat to their position, the Japanese-Americans made efforts to prove their loyalty to their adopted land. One group of Japanese-Americans in Santa Ana, California pledged funds to purchase an antiaircraft gun for the government's use in war. An antiaircraft gun at that time cost approximately $50,000.

On February 4, 1942, the Dies Committee on un-American activities announced that it would publish a "yellow paper" which would disclose the existence of a spy ring in the United States of more than 150,000 Japanese-American members. Martin Dies, the chairman of the committee, warned, "The west coast is in for a tragedy that will make Pearl Harbor sink into insignificance." Four days later the Dies Committee was recommending that all Japanese be moved from the coast. But the "yellow paper" was never published since no such spy ring existed.

The aroused and excited groups on the west coast turned their attentions to the Department of Justice and the War Department of the Federal Government in an effort to force the removal of the Japanese-Americans from the coast. The Department of Justice was subjected to strong protests from radio commentators and newspaper writers who claimed that its failure to act would create another "Pearl Harbor" on the west coast. Nevertheless, the Department of Justice stated that it was unequipped to handle any large scale movements of people over considerable distances. This left the matter squarely up to the War Department. Unfortunately, General John L. DeWitt, who was in charge of the Western Defense Command and the Fourth Army, had accepted the ideas of those who feared the Japanese-Americans. Testifying before the House Naval Affairs Committee, the general said:

> I don't want any of them (persons of Japanese ancestry) here. They are a dangerous element . . . It makes no difference whether he is an American citizen, he is still a Japanese. You needn't worry about the Italians at all except in certain cases. Also, the same for the Germans except in individual cases. But we must worry about the Japanese all the time until he is wiped off the map.

The War Department based its final decision to evacuate the Japanese on the general's insistence that it was a matter of military necessity for the Japanese-Americans to be removed from the west coast.

41

2. *Evacuation*

On February 19, 1942, President Franklin D. Roosevelt, under his authority as commander-in-chief of the armed forces, signed executive order number 9066. The order affected more than 105,000 Japanese-Americans living in the 3 west coast states. It meant they were to be uprooted from their homes and placed in concentration camps. Even worse was the haste often employed by the military units in moving the Japanese families out of their residences and businesses during the evacuation. In many instances these American citizens were given less than 48 hours to gather their possessions together for evacuation.

The evacuation of Japanese-Americans during the early months of 1942 was undoubtedly one of the darker pages in American history. Two-thirds of these people were American citizens by birth. Nevertheless, they were denied the constitutional rights of all Americans, essentially because of their race alone.

News bulletins in Los Angeles announce President Roosevelt's order to freeze Japanese assets in the United States.

Not only was the evacuation a national shame in principle, but the processes of carrying out the program of removal added insult to injury for these citizens. Those who expressed hatred, contempt, and fear of the Japanese-Americans were also the ones who gained financially from the evacuation itself. Many Japanese businessmen

Japanese-American families await evacuation from San Francisco, April 29, 1942.

had to sell their property to unscrupulous white men for 10 to 15 percent of its true value. Many farmers had to leave their crops standing in the fields and sell their farm equipment for only a few dollars. The Americans who had complained so long and loudly about unfair competition from the Japanese farmers now had their chance not only to rid themselves of the competition, but also to use this opportunity as a means of getting rich at the same time.

The government set aside some warehouses for the evacuees to store their property, personal belongings, and furniture. During the war, however, most of these warehouses were broken into by vandals and the furniture, appliances, sewing machines, ovens, and other items were stolen. Not one instance was reported where anyone on the entire west coast was prosecuted or convicted for an act of vandalism against Japanese-American property. Many Japanese signed over control of their land and business to a white American for safekeeping for the duration of the war. There are recorded instances where the white American simply sold the property and ran off with the money. Under such circumstances, it is not difficult to imagine that the Japanese-Americans were deeply hurt and quite angry about the treatment given them.

3. *Life in Relocation Centers*

The Rose Bowl in Pasadena, California is known to all Americans as a place of the Rose Parade and New Year's Day football games and other gala sports activities. Such was certainly not the atmosphere, however, on March 24, 1942. For on that morning, before dawn, 500 Japanese-Americans assembled their cars near the Rose Bowl and started a drive of over 200 miles to Owens Valley. These 500 were volunteers to go to Owens Valley Center and make it livable for other Japanese-Americans who were to follow shortly.

Upon their arrival at the Owens Valley Center, the volunteers found a desolate wind-swept camp with only 38 prefabricated barracks, a temporary field hospital, and a small mess hall and administration office. These hearty volunteers, however, met the challenge in excellent spirits. In just 7 weeks they had constructed more than 500 buildings and the population of the Owens Valley Center had grown to more than 7,000. Mr. Clayton E. Triggs, who was the manager of the Owens Valley Center, had high praise for these Japanese-Americans. He commented that they established their own "police force" and that within 7 weeks they had organized 50 baseball teams, a dance orchestra, and regular religious services. In addition, the Japanese-Americans produced their own newspaper. This was called *The Manzanar Free Press.*

The Owens Valley Center was just one of 16 temporary camps that were established away from the coast as the first location for the Japanese-Americans who were to be resettled. By the end of October 1942, all of the 16 "boom towns" had become ghost towns. The Japanese-Americans had now been moved to camps in the interior of the United States.

During this time it is interesting to note that some of the issei, or Japanese born in Japan, taunted the nisei, or Japanese born in this country. The issei questioned the nisei about the advantages of

Aerial view of a relocation camp near Parker, Arizona. Many of the camps were in deserts or swamplands.

their American citizenship. Many times the arguments that passed back and forth between these two groups caused the morale to sag considerably. The young Japanese parents with children were in a very difficult position. They had been taught by tradition to respect their parents, but they did not want their children to listen to their grandparents' influence about the treatment that was being afforded them.

The camps to which the Japanese-Americans were transferred

Evacuees boarding a train in Woodland, California.

Santa Anita race track in California was used as a school for interned Japanese children. August 1942.

were located in unsuitable climates. One was located in the desert region of Arizona and another in the swamplands of Arkansas. Other camps were placed in Colorado, Utah, Idaho, and Wyoming. When the evacuees arrived at their destination, they found that proper preparation had not been made at the camps, and living conditions were almost primitive. Sanitary facilities were lacking and the comforts of life were missing. The evacuees were greatly dismayed with this situation, but grimly went to work to improve their living quarters.

The adults elected a camp council to represent them before government authorities and submitted requests for their needs. The evacuees were restricted to these areas and could not travel freely.

The evacuation orders had forbidden them to take their automobiles with them. If they were unable to sell them, the cars had to be stored outdoors where they deteriorated very quickly. The camp councils protested bitterly but uselessly about the handling of their property. Every family lost approximately $4,000 in property alone.

The bad feelings between the issei and nisei carried over to re-location centers. In December 1942, Ralph P. Merritt, a camp director at the Manzanar Recreation Center, reported that riots had broken out between the two groups. Fred Toyama was severely beaten for being the leader of a group known as the Japanese-American Citizens League. It was necessary to place other leaders in custody for their own protection. A few days later a group of Japanese-American Boy Scouts prevented a pro-Axis group from assaulting the American flag. Undoubtedly, the concentration of more than 10,000 people in crowded living conditions kept tempers at the boiling point.

Today nearly all Americans agree that the evacuation of the Japanese-Americans was a mistake and a very serious violation of the individual rights of American citizens. Yet, in some respects, the evacuation may have been the safest procedure in view of the war-time excitement on the west coast. There were numerous stories in the newspapers accusing the Japanese-Americans of acts of sabotage 破壊 and espionage. Many local police officers reported that vigilante committees were being organized to hunt down "Japs" and kill them. Letters were written to both state and national officials demanding that steps be taken at once to prevent another Pearl Harbor on the west coast. The attorney general of California, Earl Warren, argued that the absence of any sabotage or espionage on the part of the Japanese-Americans convinced him that this was part of a plan to mislead Americans into believing that there was no danger on the west coast. Some advocated shipping the Japanese 500 miles west in chicken crates as a way of solving the problem. Even more extreme measures were suggested and given wide publicity. Some Americans who were quite friendly to the Japanese began to feel that evacuation might be the best way to protect them from the heated feelings of other Americans.

It is important to remember that there was not one single case of proven espionage or sabotage against any Japanese-American in the United States throughout the war. Yet, it was this fear of sabotage that led to the evacuation. It is interesting to note that there was no forced evacuation or relocation of Japanese living in the Hawaiian Islands during the war, even though they were 2,000 miles closer to Japan than those living on the west coast of the United States. There were three times as many Americans of Italian descent living on the west coast as Japanese, and yet these citizens were permitted freedom of movement and not subjected to any relocation process. Likewise, German-Americans were not disturbed in the exercise of their individual rights as citizens. Moreover, the Japanese had fewer foreign language newspapers being published than either the Italian or German minorities in this country. Therefore, of the various minority groups living in our nation, it was the Japanese who suffered violation of their rights as American citizens.

Lieutenant General Mark W. Clark congratulates members of the 442nd Regiment after the capture of Leghorn, Italy. July 1944.

PART V

Wartime Contributions

The episodes of evacuation and mistreatment did not create long-lasting resentment and anger on the part of Japanese-Americans toward the American people and the government. Instead, these people of Japanese descent accepted their mistreatment as a challenge, and thus won a place in the hearts of all Americans.

During the first year of the war, the Japanese-Americans had very little chance to participate in the nation's war effort. When the doors to our armed forces were finally opened to them, they took an active part in the war. In Hawaii alone, more than 16,000 Americans of Japanese ancestry were drafted into the armed forces through the selective service system. The total number of drafted men of all races in Hawaii throughout the war totaled just over 32,000. This meant that the Americans of Japanese ancestry made up nearly 50 percent of all drafted men in the territory of Hawaii during World War II.

1. *Japanese Contributions in Battle*

The most famous units of the Japanese-Americans during World War II were the 100th Infantry Battalion and the 442nd Regimental Combat Team. After the Pearl Harbor attack, the Japanese-Americans who were members of the Hawaiian National Guard were formed into a separate group. They were later sent to the United States and became the heart of the 100th Infantry Battalion. This group was first known as the Hawaiian Provisional Battalion, and it arrived at Camp McCoy in Wisconsin early in June 1942. The battalion later moved to Shelby, Mississippi, where it continued its training until August 1943.

The 100th arrived in Italy in September of 1943 and was assigned to part of the 34th Division. From September of 1943 until February 22, 1944, the 100th Infantry Battalion was in constant action. It participated in the landing at Salerno and the heavy fighting that took place there. After nearly 6 months of action in the Italian campaign, the Japanese-Americans had suffered a loss of almost 600 men due to death, wounds, or exposure.

In the spring of 1943 the government changed its policy and asked for Japanese-American volunteers for combat action in the war. The original quota was 1,500. In Hawaii alone, however, more than 9,500 men signed up for combat duty. In March 1943, 2,645 were inducted into the United States Army in Honolulu. At the same time, more than 1,000 Japanese-Americans in relocation centers in the United States had also volunteered for combat duty. These two groups were merged into the 442nd Regimental Combat Team at Shelby, Mississippi. The Regimental Combat Team began its training immediately, and after one full year of preparation for combat, sailed for Europe.

When the 442nd Regimental Combat Team arrived in Italy in June of 1944, it absorbed the 100th Infantry Battalion into its own ranks. This was a happy reunion for many members who were friends or relatives of the members of the 100th Battalion which was by now a veteran infantry outfit. The 100th Infantry Battalion had made the assault landing at Anzio Beach in Italy late in March of 1944, skirted past the capital of Italy, and was finally joined into the 442nd Regimental Combat Team.

The battalion continued its operations as the American Army crossed the Arno River after having fought and marched through the city of Pisa in northern Italy. Following this, they were pulled back from the front lines for a month's rest and in September 1944 they joined the 7th Army and its invasion of France through the south.

During this time, the 442nd Regimental Combat Team probably performed its most heroic action. This was the rescue of the famous Lost Battalion of the 36th Texas Division of the American Army. The Lost Battalion had been isolated behind German lines one week and the German high command was determined that the battalion should not be rescued whatever the cost. Since the 3rd and 100th Battalions of the 442nd Regimental Combat Team were the freshest troops in the 7th Army, they were assigned the task of rescuing the Lost Battalion. During this engagement, the 442nd lost more men than in any of its other operations during the entire war. Casualties ran as high as 60 percent, and in some rifle companies the casualties ran even higher. Ordinary infantry company strength in the 3rd and 100th Battalions was considered to be 200 men. The fighting was so heavy that many companies had from only 30 to 40 men left, and one company was down to less than 10. Some companies and platoons operated without their regular officers who had been killed or wounded, and the noncommissioned officers took over the responsibility and continued the battle. After nearly six days of terrific combat, the Lost Battalion was rescued.

German storm troopers surrender to riflemen of the 100th Infantry Battalion. Italy, July 1944.

In March 1945, the Japanese-American units departed from France and relanded in Italy. At this time they were joined to the 92nd Division. Here they fought for the rest of the war. During this campaign Sadao S. Munemori earned the Medal of Honor. Munemori was born in Los Angeles, California and volunteered as a member of the 100th Infantry Battalion. On April 5, 1945 near Seravezza, Italy, he gave his life in an heroic gesture. The army citation best describes his contributions:

He fought with great gallantry and intrepidity near Seravezza, Italy. When his unit was pinned down by grazing fire from the enemy's strong mountain defense and command of the squad devolved on him with the wounding of its regular leader, he made frontal, one-man attacks through direct fire and knocked out two machine guns with grenades. Withdrawing under murderous fire and showers of grenades from other enemy emplacements, he had nearly reached a shell crater occupied by two of his men when an unexploded grenade bounced on his helmet and rolled toward his helpless comrades. He arose in withering fire, dived for the missile and smothered its blast with his body. By his swift supremely heroic action Private Munemori saved two of his men at the cost of his own life and did much to clear the path for his company's victorious advance.

Sadao S. Munemori earned the Medal of Honor for courageous action in the Italian campaign.

Japanese-Americans of the 100th Infantry Battalion march to the front. Italy, May 1944.

The 442nd returned to the United States on July 2, 1946. On July 16, 1946, they were awarded a distinguished honor by the President of the United States, Harry S. Truman. Despite a heavy rainstorm, President Truman reviewed the proud members of the 442nd as they marched down Pennsylvania Avenue. At the conclusion of the review, he awarded the Regimental Combat Team the Presidential Distinguished Unit Citation. Then Mr. Truman stated:

You fought for the free nations of the world along with the rest of us. I congratulate you for that, and I can't tell you how very much I appreciate the privilege of being able to show you just how much the United States of America thinks of what you have done. You are now on your way home. You fought not only the enemy, but you fought prejudice, and you have won. Keep up that fight, and we continue to win—to make this great Republic stand for just what the Constitution says it stands for: the welfare of all the people all the time.

This was not the only unit citation that these two distinguished groups received during the war. In fact, they had received seven separate Presidential Unit Citations for outstanding operations and brilliant tactical operations during their months in combat in Italy and France. The 100th Infantry Battalion was correctly titled, "The Purple Heart Battalion." The individual members of the 442nd Combat Team and the 100th Infantry Regiment received more than 5,940 awards and medals from the United States Government in addition to awards to individual members from the governments of France and Italy.

The total casualties among Japanese-Americans ran over 1,700 men and officers killed and nearly 5,000 wounded in the course of the war. The battle cry, "Go for broke," became well-known to every American in our nation. The acts of bravery and valor performed by these men of Japanese ancestry have written some of the most glorious pages in our nation's history. In a sense, these brave young men were really purchasing a better future for their families in the United States through their wartime sacrifices.

2. *Contributions at Home*

While the 442nd Infantry Regiment was achieving success and acclaim in Europe, other Japanese-Americans were doing their share towards the nation's war effort. The United States Army soon found that it needed many more interpreters in the Pacific since there were very, very few non-Japanese-Americans who could speak or read the

Robert Tamura designs a cover for the unit newspaper of the Allied translator and interpreter section in Tokyo, 1946.

Teruo Temona checks the accuracy of a document at General Headquarters, Tokyo. Both military and civilian nisei made valuable contributions as interpreters and proofreaders.

Japanese language. Therefore, the decision was made to accept the nisei on a trial basis. The trial was very short because these young men proved to be dedicated Americans. They conducted themselves in the Pacific War against Japan in such a way that not a single unfavorable report was ever made about them. They soon proved themselves to be invaluable to our armed forces in the Pacific and gained much useful information by questioning prisoners.

The older generation of Japanese-Americans, the issei, were not to be outdone by the younger generation. Many of the issei volunteered to become instructors for the special language schools established by our armed forces to train Japanese interpreters. These men and women worked diligently day after day to convey their knowledge of the Japanese language to young American officers in the Army, Navy, and Marines.

In 1944 the government relaxed some of the restrictions upon the Japanese-Americans in the relocation centers. Since the war was still in progress, they were not permitted to return to the west coast. However, some were permitted to move to the Midwest. The reception they received in these new communities was not completely friendly. Within a remarkably short time, however, they gained increased tolerance from their neighbors. Their children, who were less affected by prejudice, quickly made friends with their schoolmates and generally excelled in their studies. Some were elected class officers. Others participated in sports. During the last year of the war against Japan, some young Japanese-Americans were elected presidents of their senior classes and others were chosen as the outstanding members of their school athletic teams.

Boats off Diamond Head, Honolulu.

PART VI

The Japanese in Hawaii

Hawaii is unique in many ways. It is the newest of our 50 states. It was once ruled by a queen with a name most of us cannot pronounce—*Liliuokalani.* It has a greater mixture of races and people than any other place on earth. Its climate and scenery are world famous. Most Americans dream of spending a vacation at one of its famous beaches.

Hawaii is also unique in the history of the Japanese-Americans. The Japanese-Americans make up the largest single ethnic group of Hawaii's population. In this century those of Japanese ancestry have continually made up 37 to 42 percent of the people living in the islands.

1. *Japanese Immigration to Hawaii*

The pattern of immigration from Japan to Hawaii is very similar to the immigration to the mainland of the United States. A study of the chart below will show the steady increase in numbers since the first reliable census was taken on the islands in 1890.

During the first four decades of this century, most of the immigrants to Hawaii earned their livelihood by farming or fishing. Their sampans, or small fishing boats, were scattered over wide areas of the Pacific around the islands. It was a thrilling sight to watch the fishing boats racing around Diamond Head in the early hours of the morning trying to be the first to dock at the wharves in Honolulu and thereby get the best price for the day's catch. Others turned their efforts to farming and the Hawaiian islands soon became dotted with small Japanese farms. The Japanese helped develop irrigation canals and ditches and reaped rich rewards from the fertile island soil.

Despite their large numbers, the Japanese-Americans in Hawaii never fully expressed themselves in island community life before

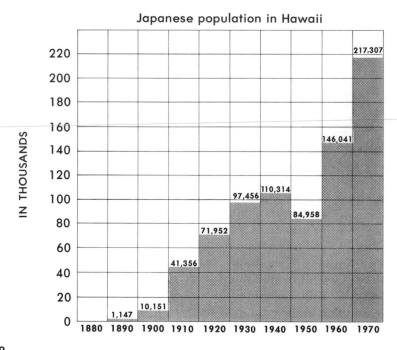

Japanese population in Hawaii

World War II. They had lived under an absolute form of government in Japan, and the ways of a democratic society were quite strange to them. Political questions were generally left to native Hawaiians and white immigrants who tended to dominate the government.

The children of the Japanese in Hawaii had to attend two schools each day. First, they attended the regular public schools and studied subjects typical of ordinary American elementary and secondary schools. After this regular school was dismissed, Japanese children went to their special school where they learned the language of their parents' native land. Many of these students later put their ability to speak two languages to good use in World War II by serving as interpreters in the United States Armed Forces. These schools, however, were disbanded almost immediately after the Pearl Harbor attack.

2. World War II

We seldom realize the great influence of folklore, legends, and myths upon our lives. Every American is aware of such characters as Rip Van Winkle and Paul Bunyan. The mere fact that there never were such individuals does not diminish the influence of these legendary figures in our history. These are harmless legends, however, and we continue to repeat the tales to oncoming generations. Sometimes, however, myths are not harmless and the constant retelling only creates further damage.

One of the most widely held myths in our country today is that the Japanese attack on Pearl Harbor was aided by Japanese-Americans living in Hawaii. After the attack, stories were told about how strange lights appeared to give signals to Japanese submarines. Another tale described how the Japanese-Americans cut their crops so that they would leave the outline of arrows pointing towards Pearl Harbor to help Japanese bombers. Japanese-Americans were said to have secret radio transmitters to send reports of our troop movements. Island fishing fleets were said to be spying on American naval movements to report to Japan. The Pearl Harbor disaster made many of these stories appear to be true and the stories grew in size and length as they were repeated over and over again.

Japanese laborers on a sugar plantation, Hawaii, about 1890.

The truth is just the opposite of those myths. After the most careful and painstaking investigations, the official reports of our armed forces and intelligence agencies reflect that there was not one single act of sabotage or espionage by Japanese-Americans in Hawaii either before Pearl Harbor or throughout the war. Unfortunately, many Americans do not realize this yet.

World War II brought many changes to Hawaii. The destruction of property during the Pearl Harbor raid was extensive. Blackouts, curfews, rationing, identification cards, and shortages of many items became commonplace. American servicemen appeared in ever increasing numbers, and acres of beautiful farmland were now used for barracks and military bases. Hawaii became the front line of our war in the Pacific, and martial law was established.

Rice fields, Hawaii. Farming and fishing were the chief occupations of the Japanese in Hawaii before the war.

Japanese-Americans in Hawaii were under a cloud of suspicion during the first months of the war. All of their radios and weapons were confiscated by authorities, and their freedom of movement was severely restricted. Gradually, however, they made a place for themselves by their contributions to the war effort. Japanese women rolled bandages and prepared medical kits for the Red Cross. War bond drives were oversubscribed in Japanese communities. Japanese volunteers for the armed forces soon proved worthy of the trust placed in them, and the absence of any espionage acts gave additional evidence of their loyalty to the United States.

Since it was felt to be unpatriotic to wear the traditional Japanese kimono, many women appeared in Western dress for the first time. Businessmen refused to conduct business in the Japanese language, and an emphasis was placed on speaking English in most Japanese homes. Some Japanese volunteered for transfer to the mainland of the United States, but the shortage of ships kept this number very low.

Thanks to the great military record of Japanese-American servicemen in both the European and Pacific theaters of war, the Japanese-Americans in Hawaii came to be regarded favorably. More importantly, they gained greater confidence in themselves and took pride in their wartime contributions. When the war was over, the man who had fought so valiantly for his country was no longer content to be a second-class citizen or politically inactive. Japanese-American candidates for political office no longer were considered rare individuals.

Japanese fishing sampans at Kewalo Basin, Oahu.

61

Senator Daniel K. Inouye.

3. *The Japanese in Hawaiian Politics*

Daniel Ken Inouye became majority leader in the Hawaiian Territorial House of Representatives in 1952. He later served in the Territorial Senate and was elected to the United States Congress in 1959 as a representative. He won election to the United States Senate in 1962 and again in 1968. In 1973, Senator Inouye played a major role in the Senate's investigation of the Watergate affair and of 1972 election campaign practices.

Daniel Inouye was born in Hawaii in 1924 and served in the 442nd during World War II. He received a battlefield commission and retired from the army a captain. The senator has a doctor of jurisprudence degree from George Washington University Law School.

Another outstanding Japanese-American leader is Masayuki Matsunaga. Matsunaga, Hawaiian-born, worked his way through college as a stevedore, warehouseman, bookkeeper, and sales clerk. He served with great distinction during World War II and twice was wounded in battle. His military medals are too numerous to mention. Matsunaga received a degree from Harvard Law School in 1951 and served in both his municipal government in Honolulu and the national government in Washington. He was a member of the Hawaiian Territorial Legislature during the 1950's and became majority leader in 1959. He was first elected to the United States House of Representatives in 1962. Representative Matsunaga was

Representatives Patsy Mink and Masayuki Matsunaga. Mrs. Mink, a lawyer, was the first woman of Asian ancestry to be elected to Congress.

once described as the most active citizen in civic, community, welfare, and veterans' organizations in all of Hawaii.

Patsy Takemoto Mink has also had a distinguished career in government. Mrs. Mink received her doctor of jurisprudence degree from the University of Chicago in 1951, and soon after that began her political career. In 1955, she was named attorney to the Hawaiian Territorial House of Representatives. The next year she was elected to that body, and for six of the next nine years she served in the Hawaiian legislature. In 1964, Mrs. Mink was elected to the U.S. House of Representatives. There she has distinguished herself as a spokeswoman for young people, women, and minorities, as well as for educational and environmental concerns. Patsy Mink was chosen Outstanding Woman In Politics in 1965, and Outstanding Woman of Accomplishment in 1967.

Senator Inouye and Representatives Matsunaga and Mink are only three of the many Japanese-Americans who have entered into Hawaiian political life. Over one-third of the Hawaiian State Senators are of Japanese ancestry. Several of them are veterans of the 442nd. The House of Representatives also has some former members of the 442nd in its ranks. Many other Japanese-Americans are now serving on local government levels and on school boards. Thus, the fight against prejudice which President Truman spoke of is being won through the leadership of these people.

This Japanese farmer wears a waterproof version of the practical *tabis* (stocking shoes) of his ancestors.

The growth of the white population in Hawaii since World War II has reduced the number of Japanese-Americans to 28 percent of the islands' total population. Over half of all the Japanese in the islands live in urban centers, where they have entered into the business community as never before. Their economic activities have changed sharply as a result of the Second World War. Their voting patterns in Hawaii since World War II show that the many racial and ethnic groups vote for the "best man" rather than a member of their own race. This is perhaps the best sign that the Japanese-Americans have truly become a part of Hawaiian society.

4. *The Life of Japanese-Americans Since World War II*

Thanks to the great contributions made by the Japanese-Americans, public opinion has become more and more aware of the serious violation of the rights of these American citizens by the evacuation order of 1942. Congress passed a law creating an Evacuation Claims Commission and directed the Attorney General of the United States to reimburse the Japanese-Americans for damages and the loss of property suffered as a result of relocation. There have been various attempts to determine the true amount of the financial losses suffered by the evacuees, and although the United States Government did pay part of the bill, it is safe to say that nearly all of the Japanese-Americans lost far more than the government repaid. Many of the evacuees had lost the titles and deeds to their property. Others could not supply the proper documents to show the value of personal property and furniture. There was no accurate way of determining how much income the families had lost during the war years.

When the last relocation center had been closed, many Japanese-Americans settled in newer areas of the United States rather than returning to their old homes. Nearly 10,000 settled in Chicago and others moved their families to cities on the east coast and in the Midwest. About one-third of the families decided to return to their old homes on the west coast and since 1946, there has been a gradual shift back to California in particular. Unfortunately, there were still some old prejudices and hatreds existing on the west coast and a few incidents occurred in which the Japanese-Americans suffered some physical harm.

Picking up the pieces was not an easy task. Most of the people had lost all of their money, and much of their property had been

Downtown Honolulu. The Japanese are the largest single ethnic group in Hawaii.

stolen by unscrupulous white people. Gradually, however, the Japanese-Americans made progress in rebuilding their lives. One happy result of the evacuation proceedings was that many Japanese-Americans came to learn much more about their new country. Those who resettled in new homes in other parts of the nation found that the prejudices against them were much less, simply because there were fewer Japanese in these areas. They also found it much easier to live according to American customs since they were surrounded by Americans.

Conclusion

The contributions of the Japanese-Americans to our country have been very great. Their industry and good citizenship are widely known to those familiar with them. They have become scientists, professors, journalists, entertainers, businessmen, farmers, and have entered into a wide diversity of occupations throughout the breadth of our nation. The behavior and conduct of their children has been exceptional and juvenile delinquency is practically unknown in Japanese-American groups. One of the most fitting statements ever made about the Japanese-Americans was written for a Mississippi newspaper:

The loyal Nisei have shot the works. From the beginning of the war, they have been on trial, in and out of uniform, in army camps and relocation centers, as combat troops in Europe and as front line interrogators, propagandists, and combat intelligence personnel in the Pacific where their capture meant prolonged and hideous torture. And even yet they have not satisfied their critics. It seems to us that the Nisei slogan of "Go For Broke" could be adopted by all Americans of good will in the days ahead. We've got to shoot the works in a fight for tolerance.

TOTAL JAPANESE POPULATION IN UNITED STATES, 1880-1970

1880	150
1890	2,039
1900	24,326
1910	72,157
1920	111,010
1930	138,834
1940	139,506
1950	141,365
1960	473,170 *
1970	591,290 *

*These figures include the Japanese population of the state of Hawaii.

In just 100 years the Japanese immigrants to our country have performed a service for all Americans. They have steadily worked hard at their jobs and learned the ways of their adopted homeland. They have suffered prejudice, insult, physical harm, loss of property, and finally the greatest tragedy of all, evacuation from their homes and placement in relocation centers. Despite these setbacks they have maintained an intense loyalty to the United States and have served all Americans well throughout the years. Certainly they have won the respect of all Americans, and through their own efforts have cast aside their second-class citizenship and assumed their position as American citizens. Their greatest service, perhaps, has been to teach all Americans that color of skin, religion, physical appearance, and language are not the true measuring sticks for patriotism.

ACKNOWLEDGEMENTS

The illustrations are reproduced through the courtesy of: pp. 6, 9, 32, 33, 35, Library of Congress; pp. 11, 15, 18, 19, 36, Toyo Miyatake, Los Angeles, 1907 Japanese Yearbook; pp. 10, 13, Consulate General of Japan, N. Y.; p. 14, Japan National Tourist Organization; pp. 17, 37, 38, 39, Independent Picture Service; p. 21, Photo Hawaii; p. 23, Minoru Yamasaki and Associates and Hedrich-Blessing; p. 24, Minoru Yamasaki and Associates and Baltazar Korab; p. 25, Minneapolis Star; p. 26, The Associated Press; p. 27, U. S. Olympic Committee; p. 28, James O. Sneddon, Office of Public Information, University of Washington, Seattle; p. 29, California Historical Society; p. 30, Underwood and Underwood; p. 42, International News Photos; pp. 43, 45 (bottom), War Relocation Authority, photo no. 210-G-2-C423 and 210-G-2-C504 in the National Archives; pp. 45 (top), 46, 49, 51, 52, 53, 54, 55, U. S. Army Photograph; pp. 57, 60 (bottom), 61, 64, Hawaii Visitors Bureau Photo; pp. 60 (top), Public Archives, State of Hawaii; p. 62 (top), Benny's Studio, Honolulu; p. 63, Office of the Senator; p. 66, Advertiser Photo.

ABOUT THE AUTHOR . . .

NOEL L. LEATHERS writes about the Japanese in America with an extensive background in history, languages, and personal wartime experiences. Dr. Leathers interrupted his college education for four years to serve in the Marine Corps as a Japanese interpreter. After the war he received his bachelor's and master's degrees in history at Oklahoma State University. He worked as a special agent for the Federal Bureau of Investigation and taught high school history before resuming studies for his doctorate, which he received in 1963 at the University of Oklahoma. His major field of study was modern European history. Formerly chairman of the history department at the University of Toledo, Dr. Leathers joined the staff of the University of Dayton in 1973. He is author of the *State Social Studies Curriculum Guide*, published by the Oklahoma Department of Education, and *French Balkan Diplomacy*. Dr. Leathers lives in Dayton with his wife and six children.

The IN AMERICA *Series*

We specialize in publishing quality books for young people. For a complete list please write:

LERNER PUBLICATIONS COMPANY
241 First Avenue North, Minneapolis, Minnesota 55401